S0-BSV-988

if only the gods were awake

Gary Girdhari

A Guyana Journal Publication

Cover Design: Gary Girdhari
                  Consultant: Catriona Shanti Girdhari-Brunelli
This book is set in Garamond
Library of Congress Control Number: 2011929490
ISBN: 978-0-615-19511-7
Printed in the United States of America

Published by Guyana Journal Publication
May 2011

105-27 Liberty Avenue
Ozone Park, NY 11417
United States of America
718-835-1530

Copyright © Gary Girdhari 2011
All rights reserved.

This book may not be reproduced in any manner whatsoever without permission.

Gary Girdhari

if only the gods were awake

Prologue

GARY GIRDHARI, a Guyanese by birth, is a retired Professor of Biology with research interests in IVF/ Embryology. He was among the first group of students selected for admission to the Faculty of Natural Sciences of the University of Guyana during its foundation year-1963, and he completed his B.Sc. with an outstanding and consistent record of both meticulous laboratory and field investigations. But Gary is remembered specially by me, one of his UG Professors, much more for his well-developed critical faculty and the breadth of his intellectual interests, qualities "which alas are all too rare among undergraduates". His abilities and research interests took him to the United Kingdom where he completed his Doctorate. He served as a Lecturer/Senior Lecturer/Head of the Biology Department at UG. Subsequently, he worked as an investigational service consultant.

Over the years, Dr. Girdhari has sustained a wide-ranging interest in the Natural Sciences, especially their impact on human life and human societies. He continues to write papers not only on scientific topics, but also insights on the problems of the Guyanese and Third World diaspora, reflections on Violence, War and Peace, and on the complex inter-relationships between ethnicity and politics in his native Guyana, with a signal desire for conflict resolution. As a humanist, Girdhari has moved away from the traditional approaches to addressing issues, and now prefers to subsume 'science' under the much broader rubric of "knowledge", trying always to establish causation as definitively as possible, rather than to be satisfied with the rash conclusions of the popular press.

As the editor of *Guyana Journal*, he has always strongly advocated, in very effective prose writings, the priority that must be accorded to grassroots and community activities, in any consideration of the problematic of Man and his Environment. His poetry is merely an emphatic and emotional extension of those prosaic utterings. These poems tell *his* story and *his* philosophy, both of which testify to the persistent memory and imagery he carries with him, of his family, siblings, parents, and special friends in the web of life.

Gary Girdhari lives in Queens, New York where, like Pablo Neruda, he seeks that balance "between solitude and solidarity, between feeling and action, between the intimacy of one's self, the intimacy of mankind, and the revelation of nature."

Harold Drayton, Ph.D.
Former Professor & Head, Department of Biology
First Deputy Vice-Chancellor, University of Guyana.

Dedication

To my parents who have conceded so much and received so little throughout their lives – lives that seemed to be filled with too much painful but dutiful work and very little joy.

To my grandchildren who give unconditional love and never ask the same in return.

To my children for whom I wish I could have done better, and with whom I should have interacted more. As mentioned in one of my poems: *If only we could go back and live and love// The clock does not reverse for anyone!*

... with the hope for humanity not held captive by doublespeak demagoguery, and not deluded by hypocrisy.

Acknowledgement

I am grateful to many individuals, which makes it difficult to list them all. Harry McD. Persaud and Balwant (Bhaggi) Bhagwandin undeniably motivated me to get the ball rolling. Gokarran Sukhdeo was always obliging in elucidating tricky construction. Janet Naidu willingly offered helpful ideas. Over the years I have received enormous gratification and support from members of the Association of Artists & Writers in Queens, New York.

Contents

Introduction

GREW UP IN A VILLAGE in Guyana where there were few if any books in the home, no bookstore, nor library. The only books children were exposed to were those prescribed by the church-controlled Success Canadian Mission (primary) School. Some parents were economically constrained, and found it an expensive luxury to purchase schoolbooks let alone any other book, prioritizing basic necessities of life instead. Also the relative low literacy level of the parents contributed to the dearth of reading materials. One or two individuals would buy daily newspapers, a few doing so ostensibly to present an air of literacy and/or civic awareness, as well as to resell for wallpapering. As children's reading skills improved, a few old tattered, dog-eared comics, such as Archie, Phantom, and cowboys, were passed around secretly as they were not considered suitable reading material.

Yet, I looked forward to attend school at the mandatory eligible age of five. (There was no nursery school, play school, kindergarten or Pre-K.) Teacher Vy (Holder) was a permanent fixture in the Prep A class which was popularly referred to as Li'l ABC. We, the tender children, learned the alphabet, simple word pronunciation, and numbers; we did drawing; we sang; and we sang-along many nursery rhymes. We did simple physical exercise; took brief naps; and enjoyed recess. There was no caning at this age, and no threats. Pre-K was happy fun learning days.

I still remember the nursery rhymes. But for the next seven years, starting from Prep B (or Big ABC) through Standard VI, schooling got progressively more harrowing, and less fun. We were compelled to learn, whether or not we had the ability and motivation, or whether or not the teachers and/or their methodologies were good or bad. Mistakes were not tolerated. (Even dirt under fingernails qualified as a mistake – in a farming community!) And the disciplinary mandate was caning on the palms or buttocks, presumably upholding the biblical (Proverbs 13:24) mandate – spare the rod and spoil the child. The physical pain inflicted did not improve academic achievement. Some pupils got more than their fair (and fear) share. And any embarrassment was mollified since it was a common experience in the open conjoined classrooms. Eventually, the pattern was set: you would know what day of the week and what period of the day to expect the caning. Thinking about it now it seems so Dickensian, degrading, and non-productive – and revolting! But this was the practice of education at the time, and it was very much entrenched in the Education Code as the norm.

Friday afternoons were a mixed blessing. Singing, sewing, woodwork, and gardening were pleasurable, but poetry time was feared. Every week there was a new poem to be memorized and recited in front of the class. Failing to perform was an invitation for the cane, the degree proportionate to the extent of the memory lapse. Many were spared the rod because they crammed well. But there were the regulars who were given the option of the palm or buttocks. After this dreaded period we luxuriated in jubilant recreational outdoor games.

I was among those lucky ones and, because I always did well when called upon, I became a favorite – among the chosen few – who were rarely called upon to recite.

Although I enjoyed most of the poems (mostly foreign

with no experiential relevance, like Lochinvar, Elegy Written in a Country Churchyard, Death the Leveller Sceptre and Crown, Leisure, A Psalm of Life, etc.) I crammed them out of fear – not wanting to be whipped. But I do not remember any now, despite their enduring quality. For the next ten years I did not read or listen to poetry. I lost the love for it. Even when W.H. Auden was introduced at university, the joy for poetry was still dormant or non-existent, although I did enjoy good literature such as Charles Dickens, Theodore Dreiser, C.P. Snow, V.S. Naipaul, Maxim Gorky, and others. However, my love for poetry and the excitement derived came back when I bought Martin Carter's slim volume *Poems of Resistance*. The power of the word, the vibrancy, and the profound message of Martin Carter stirred me immensely. I re-read *Poems of Resistance* many times – still do occasionally.

Being trained in the natural sciences, I did not write poems; I felt, subconsciously, that this was the forte of those who excelled in the languages. Around 1973/74 I was prompted to write verses – a new and exciting environment was the driving impetus – and I had the time. The many verses are lost most likely during movement. My interest faded again for more than two decades. Then during the mid-1990s I occasionally grouped with Harry McD. Persaud and Balwant (Bhaggi) Bhagwandin, and we would read poetry in a basement. Bhaggi was already an intense poet, having written hundreds, kept neatly bound. He would lead conversations on Allen Ginsberg, Emily Dickinson, Robert Frost, Ezra Pound, William Carlos Williams, Walt Whitman, and others. We also discussed many Caribbean poets such as Derek Walcott, A.J.

Seymour, John Agard, Mahadai Das, and others.

Slowly I picked up on Bhaggi's extraordinary knowledge of and devotion to poetry. And in an indefinable manner I was jolted to write. My first public reading of my own poem was done at a Canadian Writers Guild event in Queens, New York. At that event I listened to many writers. There I saw Ken Korsbie perform for the first time. I was elated and motivated.

In 1996 the *Guyana Journal* began publication; I was/am its Editor & Publisher. A Poet's Corner gave exposure to many poets, some hitherto not known for their writings. I myself have placed a few of my poems in its pages. The formation of the *Association of Artists & Writers* in Queens, New York in 1999 saw an increased interest in writing and readings.

It is obvious that different people have their own reasons for writing poetry. I write poetry because something or someone out there excites my thought processes. My poetry relates to people, matters, and things that I care deeply about. Poetry for me provides a very private space that allows freedom of imagination – to look out into the distance and marvel, and, contrariwise, to look for openings to the heart from a distance. I also feel a sense of sincerity, responsibility and honesty in poetic communication. Inescapably, I derive great joy and pleasure in the quenching of the many itchy stimuli. It is inspirational and satisfying. Presumably, there is an endorphin rush, not unlike feeding a craving. In this way, I am immersed in an ethereal solitude, that private space that provides psychological and ecstatic mental release – especially when I complete a poem.

The poems in *if only the gods were awake* were written over a period of years, some times with lavish bursts of activity, interrupted with prolonged right brain diapause. They speak to nostalgic feelings, emotions and love, nature and society, war and peace, and philosophy.

Still, I do not consider myself a poet. I follow no specific format, probably because I was not trained in the rules. I write poetry mostly for *me* – au naturale! For me, as for others, poetry is a format that allows for so much to be said in few words – with such profound and far-reaching effects – in love (Rumi, Pablo Neruda), revolutionary (Sir Walter Scott, Walt Whitman, José Martí, Martin Carter), patriotism (Aimé Césaire, Rabindranath Tagore, José Martí, Martin Carter), and many other thousands throughout the globe. Like *music, when soft voices die, vibrates in the memory*, poetry lives on for all times. For example, Abel Meeropol's *Strange Fruit* still gives me shivers, Martin Carter's *I Clench My Fist* and Rabindranath Tagore's *Where The Mind is Without Fear* strengthen my resolve. And there are many others like John Agard, Langston Hughes, and my compatriot Balwant Bhagwandin....

Inevitably, my appreciation of the arts and growing interest have inspired me to read many poets, subliminally scrutinizing different styles and techniques, which undoubtedly helped me to improve my own writings. I might even be guilty of unwitting plagiarism – the work of so many possibly unconsciously absorbed in my thoughts. Preemptively therefore, I proffer my profuse apologize if indeed this has ever happened.

Gary Girdhari
Queens, New York
May 2011

Nostalgia

Why have we had to invent Eden,
to live submerged in the nostalgia of a lost paradise,
to make up utopias,
propose a future for ourselves?
Julio Cortazar

rootlessness

I yearn for home

No where else in my heart
can replace
childhood memories
and dreams
I can only dream. Because
there is no reality in my dream
Many years ago, born there
roaming muddy dams and filthy
yards and drains and trenches
No water, no power. Yet
I yearn for home
For you cannot replace
     the memories
         of the rivers
         and the trees and birds
         of friends and simple joy
         and little things
that live on as the reality
of dreams.

Our Genip Tree

The genip tree towering
Its slender branches swaying
In the wind, its crisp leaves
Rustling tunes in the breeze.

Restless branches rubbing in gracious embrace
Messages with discordant sound
Then without a thought or a trace
My flight is upward bound.

The genip tree provides good memories
Not just its succulent berries
And pervading refreshing shade
That you never want to trade.

When you're little you take for granted
The simple board and rope swing
On the genip tree, my father constructed
Children's songs, memories and joy forever lingering.

ole time: getting ready for school

You remember... those days... before morning chores
when you'd jump-skip along the footpath
Avoiding patches of smelly   mud and grimy   water
Going for your usual bath

You remember... the break of day
when you'd join others at the waterside
Greeted by life-giving *surya*, not yet in flaming fiery fury
Wind, cool and balmy, enhanced by the fluent tide

You remember... rushing waters laced with froth on craggy seawalls
Human fixtures chewing black sage, spitting
Bare backsides hung in the distance, disguising
And many little ones in the giant Essequibo
Having their morning dip, even so

You remember... the cool brown water
Fresh, sometimes brackish, silted, washing or falling
tides that bring *four-eyes,* man-o-war, seeds of *jumbie* earring, *ite* and *mora*
Sometimes calm, kissed by a ribbon of sunlight stretched, brilliance so brazen
caricaturing a silted moustache and *crapo* beard, fit for aquatic opera

You remember... time, without a clock to see
The distance of the sun from the horizon
tells to the nearest degree

You scramble out and save your Rex or Zex salt soap
between blades of leaves
Your skin briskly dried with a towel

Surya: (hinduism) sun.

brown with age and exposure
cut from the used flour sack
Skipping over the trodden trodden track
Rinsing feet in trench water with due care
Running into the house for school clothes
Oiling han'-and-foot and hair
Gobbling without delay – cold tea, roti and curry
Looking smart – shirt in pants, hair part
moving in a hurry
Your cloth book-bag dangling as you plod your way to school
On the red-brick road, nonchalantly
Mud squish squish between your toes caressingly.

metamorphosis

while cocooned with ignorance for years
silently growing   dreaming   with unknown fears
brimming and burning with life energy
bursting out of darkness leaving only a shadowy effigy
and soaring onwards like the butterfly in spring
emerging assuredly from the embryonic soup of my being
i have come from a tiny village
some say backward and savage
they called me docile and shy
but I egged on and aimed high
some call it serendipity!

The Ploughman's Foot

You walk on the red-brick road
Barefooted
feet hardened 'gainst jagged edges
of stones and bricks.

You turn onto the foreboding backdam road
Mud squish, squishing between your toes
Big toes gnarled inwards
pressing downwards
anchoring firmly in slippery mud
Ploughman's foot
keeps balance and prevents a fall.

The brick road hot
mud   soft, cool, sensuous
Not preferred today
Nor tomorrow, nor tomorrow's tomorrow.

In the mud lurking
Imperceptible
is *kamwari* and goat *pimpla*
Tiny and sharp
Your hardened soles no match
Maga na hungry
L'il ax a cut down big tree
Safety pin in hand
Dexterity of a surgeon
The thorn removed
A-a-ah! What relief to the ploughman's foot!

Gary Girdhari

Matri Bhumi

This land of many waters
This land of many races
This land of verdant green beauty
This land of spectacular places.

This land of native peoples
Accepting others from afar, many
across the telescoping *kala pani*
Straining umbilical cultural linkages
Damned to an eternity by flawed bridges?

This land soaked with blood, sweat and tears
This land of torturers and tortured
This land convoluted in intricate webs of fears

    of 'who gon be' on top
    of insecurity of the dispossessed
    of constipation of the freedom of spirit
    of fear of catharsis of the soul
    of uncertainty in seeking forgiveness
    of unknowing the release to forgive.

This land where collective ancestral spirits roam
Without fear but with care
With pride, love and dignity,
Is the Elysium I'd proudly call home.

This land refers to Guyana

22

Ill-Legacy

Unwillingly
some of us
Willingly others
left our homes of birth
searching for a new life
in a land   strange and hostile
to provide for family   things
not available anymore in the land of our birth.
Crooks and thieves
Politicians   posturing
masquerading
cheated our people
raped our land.
Politicians for years
ignored the cry   loud and silent
of the teaming
parents and children
who left our homes of birth.
And others who could not
stayed and endured
the wrath and scorn. . .
Lost everything
love   integrity   self-esteem.

Megalomania

Perceptible
Deceptive
Imperceptible
Coercive
Alluring
Cunning
Are these qualities of a leader?

With guile
And premeditation
Arrogance and profane style
And wicked deliberation
Harnessed underlings
    fearful of exposure
    scared to disagree
In for the ride and easy pickings.

The ego swells
The eyes wander
The taste strange and grotesque
The mind perplexed
    and confused
        with longing
        and craze
The yearnings explode
In a frenzy of rage.

Inexplicable
The madness continues
On and on and on . . .
   in disquiet
   and dismay
As the country slumped in disarray.

Crazy with power
Drunk with power
Power drunk, *inter alia*
Megalomania.

I, man, says he, the king
All *your* fortunes bring
Sooner, not hereafter
Because, says he, I am the *kabaka*.

The Second Diaspora

When it started it told you not
For some, very early
Others tarried
No real cause, no special pressure
Reasons varied
Fear, intimidation, money, family
Justifiable gesture.

Tears came and pain strained
Regrets loud in secrecy
Composure regained
While others thanked the US Embassy.

We are Guyanese
from China, Madera, India and Africa
Amerindians and Europeans, if you please
But migrants twice departed
We are the second diaspora.

Pain lingers, yearning to return
To a land we dare call home
Destroyed, desecrated, isolated, spurn
    by the lunacy
Tuned to a path of economic doom
Bribery, corruption, discrimination and party paramountcy.

(1997)

The Itch

The evening cloud darkens
Masking the tired sun, blinding
The compelling yawn, overpowering
The eagle on high taunts me to follow her....

Looking For Yourself

Who am I?
As I look out
   of the window
   in the mirror
As I appear
   in the public
   at my job
As I show myself
   to my family
   and my friends
      obsessed
      naïve
      pompous
      conceited
      cunning
      discreet
Happy and willing
To please others, not myself
To gain acceptance and not be accepted
   by the public
   at my job
   by my family
   and my friends

cogito ergo sum…

Who-am-I?
My secretive Sisyphean soliloquy.

Names that stay with us

In days gone by there were
 Big By   Li'l By   Buddy By
 Li'l Son   Son-Son   Sonah
 Big Betty   Li'l Betty
 Big Gyal   Li'l Gyal   Black Gyal   Gyaloo
 Daata   Daataleen
 Maaga   Chim   Vimto   Mouse
 Johno   John-John
 Smallie   Biggie
 Baata   Brown Bear   Phantom
 Cracks   Baker   Chuchill
 Reds   Zegga   Mac
 Bigs   Barap   Bun-Batty
 Waals   Mannizing   Curry
 Pinkan   Pinky
 Baby   Baaba   Babyloo   Babyleen
 Jackoo   Zambo   Zad-a-war
 Tis   Dacta   Boom
 Pill-Pill   Big Belly
 Little Man   Feh   Tatang
 Duff   Moutie   Putagee   Coolie-maan
Not forgeting
 Dry-carn   Boo-Boo   Bundha   Pack-Pack

Musical false-names without rhyme   that
stay with us all the same.

of old age

alone
smothered
   by songs
      of old men
where the vibrancy
and the lusciousness
      of flowers
and
      the eyes of women
are lost in dreariness.

betrayed

to sit and mope
as days wear away
with sanity saltating in dismay
is like moments of time delayed
the feelings of one betrayed.

Gary Girdhari

Now is the time

If only we could go back
and live and love…
The clock does not reverse for anyone!

32

My Dear Cheddi

It's now many, many a day
Since that fateful moment
When friends and foe alike
Listened in dismay
That your final breath
Was snapped away.

Many say it's official
To end the period of mourn
But
Nay, your sojourn
Sadness, grief, love
Nostalgia
An abiding peace full of pain
To know with sure belief
That your fight is not in vain.

'Tis the reason for our strength
To think of that sad time and the future bright
Knowing that *everything will be all right.*

(06/28/1997)

Cheddi and Janet
(In Memory)

Cheddi and Janet, Janet and Cheddi
A clear vision in their mind   steady
Together they formed the invincible duo
Bringing Guyana out of a system eons ago.

A young couple with perpetual dream
Devotion applied, never out of steam
To work hard and long among the mass
To remove them from their plight and political morass.

Idealist fervor harbored in their mind
As they studied and learned of humankind
Ideals full of magnanimity and devotion
Practiced throughout their lifetime in the nation.

Meeting in Chicago, USA
Married and moved to Guyana without delay
Embarked on a task with no ifs or buts
What they did took lots of guts.

Remember . . . they
Tireless, fearless, frontier spirit   not squeamish
Decidedly took on the mighty British!
Just out of their teens and into their early twenties
Most certainly battles fought from the trenches.

Fed up, some say, 'Twas better under Her Majesty
'Cause their lives got worse under party paramountcy
But Cheddi and Janet, Ashton and Joycelyn started something new
At first, their friends were few.

First to topple the status quo
Idealism their motivation   underestimating their foe
In for battle with the powers that be
A will to succeed, the original four with leader Cheddi.

Idealism and ideology   and a claim
To wrest Guyana from slavery called by a new name
Colonialism, a system of subjugation and exploitation
Sucking the blood of people and the nation.

Think about it . . .
How would you feel
If some one makes a deal
To control your house   your family   your life?
An outsider that doesn't belong   creating strife?

You lose your honor and self worth
Assuredly, from the time of your birth
Your *self* disavowed, replaced by values new
Foreign in concept   the red-white-and-blue.

The fact . . .
You're taught to hate your own
Later in life you bemoan
You lose your religion and your name
You bow to *bakra*   the *massa*   with shame.

In school you must sing God save the King (or Queen)
Learn British history and geography and everything in between
Insidiously, you despise your race, your color and value system
Taken over by another, creating confusion and problem.

Remember . . . also
Your Majesties, Governors: Lethem, Woolley, Savage, Renison, Grey
All you could do is   pray
Luyt, and their local yes-men
Intolerably, your country ruled by them.

Remember . . .
Government was nominated, not elected
Big business, the professions, the upper class selected
If you're White, you're all right
If you're Black, stay back.

Now, Cheddi and Janet had to fight
The entire British might
And in Guyana, many a surrogate
The working class, their duty to subjugate.

Rupert Tello, Rahaman Gagraj, James Ramphal, Joseph Luckhoo
To get by depends on who knows who
J.B. Singh, Anthony Tasker, R.E. Davis. W.O.R. Kendall, Sugrim Singh
Govern they did – the good life for the upper class did bring.

Think about it . . .
Very young people trail-blazing with the PAC
Little thought for the niceties of diplomacy
Organizing to learn, learning to organize
Writing, talking the cause to politicize.

Then was born the PPP with mass appeal
With lofty aims, no ignoble deal
Men and women, their collective wisdom
Dedicated to the cause of freedom.

Cheddi, Janet, Forbes, Rai, Hubbard, Wilson, Benn, Ramkarran
Chase, Jacob, King, Carter, Chandisingh, Ramsahoye, Nunes, Mann,
    Fred Bowman
Some with opportunism and some with guile
The façade always there, always with a smile.

Glory days gone and prison a new abode
For many stalwarts the fight went to the road
The mood sanctified in *Poems of Resistance*
Galvanizing their will in defiance.

But . . .
Treachery is not something new
The threat of prison and lure of power affected a few
Dishonorable men with greed in their sojourn
Manipulated others and were manipulated in turn.

Guyana became worst for it
Economic, social, moral and spiritual deficit
A period of history you cannot let
Any decent Guyanese forget!

Meanwhile . . .
Cheddi and Janet and the PPP on guard
Knowing the struggle will be long and hard
But win they will as they abide
Aware that both history and time is on their side.

Win they did, the glory days regained
The will to see Guyana free retained
The task to rebuild ever so clear
The challenge, a love affair so dear.

His demise premature
A legacy of truth, bread and justice for sure
For Janet, the task is always there
To uphold the legacy, and the love they share.

(11/16/1997)

Icons of Peace
(A Dedication)

Peace at last   peace forever
Should be the clarion call
Voices should resound with wondrous endeavor
Singing the melodies of peace for all.

Civilizations have come and gone   fleeting
With Nations and peoples fighting
Destroying, humiliating others with their might
For it's their doctrine that might is right.

Mohandas Gandhi was a man of peace and love
Cheddi Jagan, a man with a burning desire
'Gainst injustice, casteism, racism, imposed from above
The twain sustained their belief and dreams to the final pyre.

Gandhi remembered and Jagan   forever sure
Will live on and endure

The passing of time, today and all tomorrow
From their lives, their teachings we shall always borrow.

Gary Girdhari

Lamentation

The Flight …
Freedom in Exile
A Sad Return to My Birthplace
Giving and Forgiving
The Power of Morality and Patience
With Mindfulness and Wisdom
Creating an Enlightened Society.

(I have given a name to these literal titles from Nawang Khechog:
Quiet Mind (Tibetan Meditation Music) and I call it a poem.)

40

Emotion
Love
Regret

However long the night, the dawn will break.
Nobody really cares if you're miserable,
so you might as well be happy.
African Proverb

Gary Girdhari

The Festive Season

It's nearing winter
Leaves   almost gone
Insects   hardly
Birds   southward beyond

Cold streets are bare of people

A time of gloominess...
Till the festive season
when snow portending gladness
reflecting the lights of joyousness
and the moon for good reason

A gaiety of snowy freshness and cheerfulness enter
engulfing and enveloping the mind
with mirth and warmth in winter
giving joy and serenity in the land of slumber
and peace and love to all humankind.

my yoga

confidence and self-esteem
muscle and stamina   redeem
prana   energy   enthusiasm
chi   concentration   awakened
mental weight   lightened
peace of mind   wellness
a feeling of goodness

tormented

maybe
'twere better not to
live in imagination
    tormented
      soliloquizing innermost fantasies…
try to sleep instead. invoke morpheus
and hope to dream of the good memories

In My Heart

I always feel you are special
and care for you a lot
We are supposed to be just friends
but I feel it stronger in my heart

You have the cutest smile
a very naughty laugh
to me you are always sweet and kind
I am never awake too long without you on my mind

Even though you are distant
you must understand what's in my mind
you are very easy to engage   and kind
I wish that's how it could stay forever

I always want to tell you
how much you really mean to me
I can't find the right moment
Is this how it's meant to be?

Now I feel a closer closeness
even though our distance is wider
Why are we still far away
from the point of nowhere, today?

Though you'll never know, how much
I've cherished every moment with you
A special person with celestial aura
Tell me that you love me as I do.

45

Kid Sense

She looked at me. I still see her face
no expression
Prescience
she knows
She'll miss me
she knows
The kiss on her cheek evoked no response
I waved from the car, still
no expression
She did not smile
She did not cry; yet
Maia's silence tells me
she knows.

1998
(Written at JFK)

Still searching

A heart desperately
seeks solace
today
Finds it in the countenance
that asks
askance. Will it ever be?

It *is* the question.

The answer, sweet love, is in the stars.

Detached

why don't you feel the pain
as I do?
the child cries for attention

shadows crawl
in the grayness of night
forever and always
all ways and always

you do what's painless
inert
a clinical dreamer
detached

before me and behind me
the owl, the memory and wisdom
and now
completely detached.

Lament of a Migrant I

Heartbeat imperceptibly incrementally pacing
An overpowering shroud of dullness
An insufferable depressed feeling
Momentarily wafting you on the wings of helplessness.

You know that you're not alone
   here in New York
Many compatriots in silence bemoan
Lost years, unrecovered   productive   years of play and work
Helplessly, sinking in the sofa of complacency.

Nostalgia   calling
   and beckoning
Mind wandering through the cyberspace
   of memories and *the* place . . .
Quickly, reality evaporating the clouds of wishful thinking.

Lament of a Migrant II

A cloud of darkness engulfed his mind
Hiding tiny strands of light
Forcing through confused grey cells
Breaking a bridge between his sanity and reality.
Head in submissive incline avoiding eye contact
He glanced at me furtively and away
Facial muscles visibly tightened
And a smile, dry, spread across his face
   a vain attempt to mask a troubled mind
A disguise, hidden so poorly, obvious
   only as a cover-up
To appease my silent concern.

Doleful eyes
A plea for recognition
   of his circumstance
   of his mingled emotion
      for sympathy and empathy
Haunted eyes   insufferable angst
Consumed with worry and concern
   for family
      dislocation
      disruption
      separation
      degeneration
Eyes that speak a common language, in supplication
Was it worth it?
Is it ever worth it?

Bonding

The cardinal visited with a song
Colorful, bright and frisky   that day
Waiting for you to say
Love is life-long!

Gary Girdhari

Pleading

Wine-ing one Sunday night. Confrontation
A feeling of tenseness
in your presence
In haste, ruffled and mad
the meeting, fleeting, departing   soulmates
leaving
that freshness, restfulness and glow

lingering wariness
seeks your dispensation
of generosity and kindness

Time will tell   the proven
genuineness of my plea
When treasured special closeness
do not become illusory and stolen
for un-forgiveness.

Reconcile

Tonight

I write
To let you know the flowing
tides of feeling
that torment me now

Yesterday…

The vein on my head amplifies
Flushness of explosive corpuscles
Tension creeps up stealthily…
Imperceptible   growing steadily

Mark my word
It's not good
Control it, now: is my admonition

I try – coming to terms…
I fail – to reconcile…

Death will approach one day. Like Icarus
Still unable to control the corpuscles. But
For now
The sweet venom persists.

Feelings Suppressed

It's not nice to feel helpless
With this relentless pain
In your groin, belly, chest and brain
It's a powerful thing
This attachment, you say
You do not bring
Into the fore of life's foray

True Love

Why shouldn't I fall in love
with someone new   I stop to think.
My heart tells me a story
that my brain
fails to understand. Defies synchronicity
Poets of yore
write their stories
for millennia, not to bore.
This is my story
of love undiluted – true love
rare, ever present, rarely discovered
comes from the heart.
True love
Comes from the heart.
Even when we depart.

Gary Girdhari

Resolve

Yesterday you came
Happy, but for
 the strain in your eyes
Light conversation
 of no avail
A pretend smile showed
 your pain, pained
Mind upset not disguised by the expression
 in your eyes
The passion and the heat
 could not negate primal power. So it seemed
It's closing in. Feelings low – frustration, depression
The internal turmoil
 makes strategizing difficult
  to resolve the dilemma
The desire craves
 a strong and comforting friend
  to spend every moment
   to the end
The window of opportunity
 is now
  to reconcile
   the tingling emotions
and allow dreams
  to become real when you wake up
as with Cupid's magic wand
Quintessential peace and happiness radiating through your being

the essence
> of your own bliss
> your rapture, smiling
> your grace
> your love
>> the positive tides of life.

Those Eyes

I held your hands
Feeling warmth and tenderness
Avoiding your fiery eyes
Fire   intenseness
in your eyes
An ocean cannot quench.

I do not want to see tears
anymore
that once welled
tears that an ocean
may fill
my heart with sadness
and sweet pain.

Restless

I am awake at 2:30 am
At 3:30 I'm sipping tea
Thinking of you

Thinking of you
I read the *Gitangali*
Tagore's offering to the Creator
to soothe my heart
torn with a blissful misery
of not being able to touch you
now

The cup of tea, chilled
the hour draws high
I stare on the wall, unfilled
Imagining Mirabai
Thinking of you

Thinking of you
I ruminate
Am I out-of-date?

Yearning

Creeping through my window   the dawn light
    stealing my reverie
and the enchantment of lingering fanciful flight
    of your visage
            and your energy   captive
                    in my heart and my inner sight
Oh! the yearning
Oh! the nearness
so distant tonight

Comfort

Today, in your presence
looking at you, and feeling
your *sakti* and closeness
induced a comfortable sweetness
in my heart, to mollify a situation...

Sakti or Shakti: (Hinduism) sacred cosmic energy or force.

Game of Love

Is there a game of Love where all are defenseless?
How can sanity prevail
    in a mind made malleable?
How can you expect my mind
    to be chained?
Oh, how I wish I could be
    on your street
        with bridled eyes glued to your window
        waiting for a glimpse of your radiance.

(Influenced by Jalal ad-Din Rumi)

Fantasy

I hope I don't tire you
with my constant outpouring
   of emotions. I must say again:
   I love you
      and want you – it hurts.
Your words now have meaning to me
silently, I savor ecstatic fantasy
     of being with you…

The Disconnect

the day   mild and pleasant
easy going
no pressure
a short walk
smiles and laughter
small talk
meaningful undertones
a gentle touch   now and then
deliberate or not
in the right spot
at the right times
a stolen kiss
heart pounding
out of control
and yearning
    and yearning
        and yearning
what more to ask for...?

And then... the calm...
    Disconnect
      Love
              Despair
                    Pain
                          Reality

I wash my hands, contemplating
Ovid's farewell muse.

Empty Soul

Sometimes
I think of the days
Before I met her
When my soul was free. Free
    but empty and wanting
Like a well-fed bird in a cage.

2 Hearts Together

Masking streaks of gray
Your hair; mine already white
Our hearts are entwined, tight
Loose not the knot, I pray.

Concern

Immersed in my thought
of the delightful anger, brought
by tonight's damning droplets
I think of someone special
who is not here.

Gary Girdhari

Like the Spent Arrow

Wishing you were here   is a comforting refrain
Tonight   in close delusional embrace
I imagine a ripe maiden, sweet and kind
walking in the rain. Drenched
in a wet T-shirt
Steps already taken, difficult to retrace
Tho you're always in my mind.

Adieu

I wandered   indecisive
Glancing at your window
Uttered no sound   pensive
Sat on your chair
Gawking at your rug   fumbling adieu
Wondered if you care
Freedom is a bird soaring in the air.

Purity

this night, with the rains
comes a purity
that washes away ugly thoughts
bringing peace and sanctity
like being alone with you in a virgin jungle.

Nature's righteousness

I listened to the raindrops
saturating my mind with goodness. I bow in obeisance
I must not be alone
to absorb nature's righteousness.

Illusion

that autumn when the moon was red
nestled on your bosom
is but a mirage
conjured in a mystified dream.

The morning after

Curled like a fetus she reposed. I watched her
silence, satisfaction, completeness. Purusha and Prakriti
The storm   the calm
The sun rose too early that morning.

Purusha: (Hinduism) cosmic man
Prakriti: primal force of creation

Rapprochement

First Touch
Almost A Whisper
Before I Go
In The Morning Light
New Beginning
Nostalgia
Only A Memory
Reflections Of Passion
Sadness Of The Heart
One Man's Dream
Swept Away
Until The Last Moment
Standing In Motion
Whispers in the Dark
Love Is All

(I have made up this poem using the some titles of Yanni's music.)

Nature & Society

Humankind has not woven the web of life.
We are but one thread within it.
Whatever we do to the web, we do to ourselves.
All things are bound together.
All things connect.
Chief Seattle

My Back Yard
(in New York)

Brown gray earth
dirt
Grass green
birds preen
Butterfly
up to the sky
Lady bug
early slug
Flowers
brilliant hue
never, never too few
Bora
bigan
pakchoy, chowrai, mustard
collectively callalloo
Sage, thyme, mint, parsley, oregano
mixed in with luscious tomato
Corilla, cucumber, zucchini
cooked anyhow
with hot roti and achar bilimbi.

I love my garden
I love my back yard
It's a joy to see
the flowers open
the birds chirp and sing
the bees buzz
What pleasure these simple things bring.

Faces

Faces
Black, brown, white
All shades
All races.

Faces, faces
Round, flat, long
All shapes
All traces.

Faces, faces, faces
Blank, pained, smiling
All moods
All in good graces.

A narrative is told
From each crease and fold
Every muscle from cheek to eye
Tells stories that belie
The inner workings of the mind
And emotions of every kind.

Pretty, smiling and delicious
Sometimes but not often vexed
A scorn, a smile, rarely vicious
Reveals a syndrome perplexed.

Faces, faces, faces, faces
Everywhere you turn
The more you learn
There is no real difference among races.

Their Flowering Faces

If you want to
    love
        people and animals and the Earth
sit on your sidewalk, like me…
Look out, but *see*
There is hardly any hurting hate
    on the faces I see
Tired, maybe
Frustrated, maybe
Concerned, maybe
Wanting-to-go-home, maybe
But I *see*, no hate
    in that malleable matrix of
        tiredness, frustration, and concern
I *see*, love
    unadulterated innocence I *see*.

I look I *see*
    their flowering faces
    their eyes in acknowledgement
A simple smile
Or a wondrous word. Enough
From a shrouded stranger
    to say
        I love you
Through the indivisible invisible aura
And me
demurely smile say
    Je t'aime aussi

Ergo, I… am… always in love.

The Age of Youth

I look at them – their verbal crudity
and burn inside
But maybe
　　That's what's happening in them.

I look at them – their callousness
and turn away with scorn
But maybe
　　That's what they're displaying.

I look at them – their foul behavior
and revolt comes readily
But maybe
　　That's what they're doing.

I look at them – full of youth and life
admiring with love and recognition
Maybe
　　That's all they need.

If

If I were an adult
I'd do the right thing
That would bring
Praise, not insult.

I would not smoke
'Cause to my health
It's no joke.

Drugs I won't take
Liquor I won't drink
'Cause the day after
I'd remember how I stink.

I'd keep my home clean
My yard beautiful
The air serene.

I'd respect the air
Water
Mother earth
'Cause from these come all birth.

I'd respect my parents
My brothers and sisters
My children and grandchildren
My friends
And everyone

For without respect
There's no adoration.

I'd try not to pollute the natural beauty
'Cause it's my sacred duty.

I'd tell everyone at school
The Mayor, the Governor, the President
   Don't be a fool
   It's not cool
   To destroy our Mother
   To look for the fast buck and gain
   That children to come must bear pain.

If I were an adult
I'd do things right
And never poorly
I'd lead by example
Never to say, "For adults only."

Trapped

Getting up at 5 or 6
A hurried breakfast or not
The kids sound asleep
No time for a good-bye kiss.

The subway or bus I must get
The 7:30 or the 7 o'clock
Otherwise my pay they dock.

I am smart I know
But at work I dare not say
What's to be done any day.

I work like an animal or robot
No ideas, no brain, no thought
About what I do
Day by day
Or about my measly pay
'Cause I'm afraid to lose
Even the pittance in the envelope
On the welcome Friday.

Getting home by 6 or 7
My apartment feels like heaven
My children   did they eat?
No time to chat
Tired
Almost time to sleep.

Today, tomorrow, and so it will be
In this confounded prison
To drive this mindless economy.

Thus it was then
Thus it is today
Caught up in a system
A rat race, deplored
Forever, forever
Imprisoned!

Lost in the System

I was just going out of the door
   is the familiar lying excuse
The telephone rang
   Hello! How are you? How's everything?
     Oh! I'm busy.
The telephone rang
   How are things?
     O.K.
Can you give me a hand. . .
   I can't make it
     I'm so busy.
Can we go to the park? asked my wife
   Can't you see
     I'm busy.
Please look at my homework.
   Not now, son
     I'm busy.
Let's go to the beach
   Another time, my child
     I'm busy.
One day
It was *soooo* quiet
The phone stopped ringing
My wife stopped talking
No bother from my children
I'm all by myself
   Peace at last?

Now...
I am all alone
It's too quiet
Please, let it ring again
Please
speak to me.

I did *everything*
I worked so hard
All is lost
All in vain
In the end
Lost!
No family no friend.

This Land of Plenty

They come in hundreds of thousands
To this acclaimed land of plenty   and cold
Backs to the walls   with bloodshot   tears
Motivated   and bold
To catch up for lost years.

At first excited   playing out the stories told   when
Stretched by colorful imagination. Then
   unsuspecting
Society takes control
   of you
    your tradition
    your food
    your dress
    your speech
      of your work
          in New York
Aye! your culture…
Until you're consumed by the ultimate vulture.

Then   one day
Haunted by internalization
Like a divine inspiration
Questioning your existence in the constricting web
Remembering loved ones in a land distant   and forsaken
Regretting the cracked linkages   sometimes broken…

Your forerunners told you so
You did not believe – did not want to believe
Now *you* tell *them* – not to deceive
They do not believe
They still come in hundreds of thousands
To this land that relentlessly commands.

Gary Girdhari

We Are ~~Not~~ Involved!

Help!
We hear the call loud and clear
and keep away because of fear
Peering through curtain and blind
pulled ever slightly, the wife or husband standing behind
still, as we hear the call
Help!

The child comes to the door
"We are selling candies for our school."
"Not today," we say, eyes to the floor
with shame and feelings disgraced
But knowing horror stories of candies laced
wisely ignored the request for
Help!

There on sidewalks, streets, the subway
begging and cajoling, aggressively or in dismay
Their eyes tell their individual story
    of hurt, abuse, poverty and worry
We look away elusively, to avoid
    to sanitize our actions and minds, devoid
        of the responsibility for those seeking
Help!

Life goes on. They remain perpetually
    fixtures on our landscape everyday
1% at the top say they will go away eventually

90% at the bottom hope and pray: "I. Me,"
may never have to lament for
Help!

Today it's him or her
     friend, stranger or neighbor
Tomorrow it may be me
It's not that we do not care
It's the reality of a fear
     of repercussion, threat, retribution, or a telephone call
          that prevents us to be involved
               when we hear the plea for
Help!

They fail themselves, family, friends; with tears
Self esteem eroded lost over the years
The bottom 90% swelling, the 1% smiling
The in-between surely disappearing
Less government some demand
while the plight of the wretched gets out of hand
Charities are larger, churches ask for more.
But . . .
Neither government, charity or church cures the growing sore
     that grows bigger
          yearning for responses to the cry for
Help!

Rain

Tonight
Like the other night
Rain Rain Rain
Rain   water
Rain Rain Rain
Rainwater

Under my roof it shoots
onto my skin
feels the cool life of water

The cacophony of raindrops
like a broken necklace of pearls
dancing on clear glass
incessantly   drowning all other sounds
and all reality   but
for my visage of you
as a veiled backdrop
in the semi-darkness

Rain is water
Rainwater
Sustenance of life
Giver of life

Tonight
the lightning has gone elsewhere

but
the subliminal glow
festooning above
the branches
shows
the light   always
ever-present light   also giver of life

Rain is water
Rainwater
soft but with power
tasteless but sweet
the universal solvent
the sustainer of life
Nature's primordial sweet ambrosia

Gary Girdhari

Nature's Enigma
(Knowing constancy, the mind is open.
With an open mind, you will be openhearted. — Lao Tzu)

In ceaseless torrents it pours
and the boughs protest
the winds, competing for recognition
Sporadic lightning glows
deep in the horizon
An occasional thunder timidly
roars

Aye! the complement of Nature
or Nature's compliment!

A solitary drop tinkles
    the tin can
A niggling caution...
    in the symphony
    of life – id est
    the individuals make up the orchestra…

A selfish nabob I am too, to
    experience my intimacy
        with this quotidian nightly embrace

The dinner-bell – vittle – *vivere*
The temporal satiation
    dulls my wandering rumination

The visage remains
   steady and faithful
      like the rains tonight
ushering the wholesomeness of Nature. Life
   is sustained
      in enigmatic constancy.

Gary Girdhari

Identity

Tonight

I must be awake
I cannot go, nor parry
The rains come
The lightning continues, angry
sky with an ominous glow

Rain is water
In sheets it patters
on the roof overhead
Not the *pita-pata* onomatopoeic musical flutters

Rain – not individual droplets, but
thousands of tiny diamonds   jittering
falling asynchronously on roof top
utter the sound of elusiveness   double-dealing

One drop perceptibly drums
on the tin-can   drip-drop
Again, and again, and again   hums
Alerting me of its presence. Stop!

Is it the drop?
Or the coalescing of droplets
to create the drop?
Or is it the tin-can that demands
its presence felt?

Cell Phone Syndrome

An aching ear?
A tooth ache?
I wonder
Looking near
And yonder
Out of the subway
Out of the bus
From a hard day
Into the car
Even if near or far
Walking
Smiling
Talking speaking
Frenzied soliloquizing
Unhinging unsettling...
Like the *acushi* in a flurry
With one-track focus
They scurry
New acquired hand-neck deformity?
A vision of mass conformity?
Communication technology
In business or idle babble
Here to stay
So they say
Even for babblers just out of the cradle
At work
At home
Local
Or roam
Now diagnosed: the cell phone syndrome.

Gary Girdhari

De-Greening the Planet

Look into the distant sunset
and early sunrise morn   *Surya* salutation
The vast expanse of the oceans
Clear blue sky. Listen
    the music of streams rippling constantly
and birds and squirrels and insects
    playfully
    foraging for self and family
The circadian rhythm
    of night and day
The sun and moon and stars
    that light
        our day and night

Why do we attempt
    to kill it?
That which Nature provides for all
    the Plants
    the Animals
    Oceans and Rivers
    Stream and Air
        with our greed
                and action in abandon cavalier
We exploit our Nature
Determined as we are
    under no duress
Killing ourselves in the process.

Civilized Bondage

twisted passages of time
warping inexorably
asynchronously
   evolving in geometric progression
   helped by $e = mc^2$
offering civilized fruits   caressed so dear
creating this planet with less care
destroying   polluting   causing despair
cause we do not care
nor want to share

twere better to be blind
and not see things unkind
twere better to be deaf
and be left
bereft
   of evil machinations
   of destructive forces
   of hate generated
       to satiate ever demanding thirst
the unrestricted greed
the uncontrollable lust.

in the name of god

we fool ourselves
don't we
in the name of god

sanctimoniously
   we walk
      with heads high
aloof and aloft
nose tilted   toffee nose
greater and better
than the *others*
in the name of god

listen to the music   the *raaga*
the melody of eternity
immortal
the archetypal ultimate coexistence
     of time and space and being
in the amorphousness of energy pervading the world
that some believe is here for personal use
not understanding it is here
   not for us   but we are here for it
and
don't we not forget as the neocons and the coalition
     of the willing
  are
     now forgetting…

that god does not listen to the rich only
and cannot be bribed
    by eloquence
    and the veneer of affluence
which is not affordable to those without eloquence
who do not possess the means to bribe man
or god whom he fears

why invoke the name of god falsely
to do the dirty work
in the name of god!

Gary Girdhari

Duplicity

aphorisms
with
perverse inflections ...
sarcasm   and
cynicism
derision   and
euphemism
liberation   and
freedom
media manipulation
   called
      public relation
serving
double-speak leaders.

Johnny

Johnny is a faithful workman
for many years, he toils
in that sweltering warehouse, where
many like him, of color and accents
do the grudging work, non-stop
like the conveyor belt, can't take a break, 'cause
they look at you – the boss-man
and big brother, watching
inside your mind and belly. But you hold
the job, packing, sweeping, loading; and learn
how to escape the eyes. Keep smiling
obsequiously with practiced subservience.
Friday afternoon, they call a meeting –
things getting slow. Johnny feels his blood
rising; palm warm and moist
belly rumbling. Johnny sweating, tightens his buttocks
firm, fearing he may pee or shit his pants…
here Johnny, your check. We'll call you.
Monday morning, still at home. Never
in eleven years! He feels out of place
we going to be OK, Johnny. We gonna make ends meet
his wife, still working. Minimum wage
can't make ends meet. Hassles from four children
growing, hands and mouths open, like nestling birds.
Johnny trying – one week, two weeks, three weeks
nothing coming his way. Frustrated
pain, growing anger, eyes blank and wild. Johnny worked hard

did no wrong, to anybody. To everybody
he was a good guy. Old lyrics trickling through his mind
I feel so breakup, I want to go home.
One morning Johnny was in the line
with other indigents, on the sidewalk
near that church – dutifully – for onions, apples, potato
disregarding disgrace and shame
if people – family, friends, his children
see him and cast blame. He will say:
I keeping me friend's company.
Johnny come home. He dodged…
it's only the car stereo. Relief but queasy.
In the line Johnny had time. To think
about the trains always dirty, not on time
losing money. But the bosses get more of the gravy
about Wall Street and big Banks
ruining the economy. But getting huge bailouts
the bosses too with bonus and bigger salary
about the City, Albany, Washington DC
run-down government, budget deficit. Double-speak solution –
layoffs to solve it. But the *jefes* have the good living
they don't get fired for screwing up and wrecking the country
they don't go to jail 'cause they're too big to fail
instead they have a hearing, all dressed up. A sham
then a slam-bang, with lavish parties in the White House. Protocol?
and the Congress and Senate. Hey!
they vote their own pay raise and health insurance!
yea! republicans and democrats, no time for the peon
they're two sides of the same coin. And let's not talk

about oil spill and environment. Or sanitation and snow
the cover-ups work, the less you know.
So, don't bother about the existentialist crap
pulling up your own bootstrap. Poor Johnny
has to tie his waist. So tight
to help out with his gloomy plight
picking up cans and bottles. The crumbs from tables.
Johnny still waiting… waiting alone
The car blurted again. He joined in: *I wanna go home.*

in submissive docility

Culture is everything. Culture is the way we dress, the way we carry our heads, the way we walk, the way we tie our ties … it is not only the fact of writing books or building houses.

– Aimé Césaire

nostalgia   the fascination and   fear-full
of pained memory

a life forgotten   once
full   of living culture
a life diminished   now
to re-discover

painful then
gathering flawed messages along the way
films imported
new and improved treatments   in magazines
and *me*   aping cowboys   in the mental fray
clothes and styles
cigarette betwixt fingers
and mesmeric smiles
manly i thought
cause it looked *so o   o   o*
so machismo
a titer of placebic testosterone
naïve simpleton
pitiable icon
a sad state
determining *my* fate

poor colonials
duped into accepting *their* values-less
under benign coercive duress

still duped
into submissive docility
colonial mentality
emasculating   time
honored religion and language
a new dress code
proper and   suffocating
forces of cultural attrition
and psychical transformation
engineered to erode

now!

unashamedly denuded
in supplicated obeisance   and obedience
outdoing the masters
forsaking ancestral memories
negating cultural salience

asunder *my* soul do rent
with cultural dismemberment

PICASSO: GUERNICA

War & Peace

*When I declare that I am for peace and not war, I believe that this is a
righteous stance. I believe that this is a godly act,
not unpatriotic. We must not assume that war is inevitable.
If there is war, it signals failure of the collective wisdom of humanity
and condemns us, our civilization into abomination and oblivion.*
Gary Girdhari

Amygdala Vibration

Pathway to Peace
Happiness Together
Resonance Within
Relax
Floating With The Clouds
Silences
A Meeting by the River
Sweet Longings of Love
Remembrance
Harmony and Symphony

Floating With The Clouds
Silences

In The Gentle Rain

(These lines are titles from: Vishwa Mohan Bhatt's *Music for Relaxation*. I gave a title to make up a poem.)

Order & Disorder

Yesterday, I saw the first faint
new moon. The slim crescent hanging loosely
Boomeranging its
clean power and potency
Silvern, simple, serene
'Midst the ventriloquistic noise-i-ness
of evening cicadas
Incessantly and monotonously, penetrating
my ears
Bringing awareness:
Amidst the quiet, the clear, the pristine
Is also a world full of unrest.

(In memory of the victims of 9/11)

A Prayer

This night as I lie down to sleep
I pray the Lord my soul to keep
If I should die before I wake...
I pray that the bombs
Don't make the skies opaque.

When will the bombs stop?

the eerie silence   just before
the bombs   deafening
the lone eagle on high inspects
the aftermath of destruction.

"War. War. Everywhere is War"
(Bob Marley)

It's a bloody bloody mess
In Guyana
Iraq
Varanasi
Here and there and everywhere
Eruption of violence
Making no sense
It's fashionable to shake the rattle
To do battle
In Agricola
With no positive response but palabra

What a mess!
A bloody bloody mess!
Children of these lands everyday
Know no other way
They are born in violence
What is their future
If they know nothing else?

Listen to a man of real valor
Gandhi:
> *Liberty and democracy*
> *become unholy*
> *when their hands*
> *are dyed red with innocent blood.*

See how they brainwash:
  Pray, dear children of the flock
  Devotees of the churches
  Your blessing will overflow
  The more you tithe
  And the less you know
  So it is written
  In the good book
  Lest you be smitten
  Just give, don't look

And when you hear them say
"We are spreading peace and democracy"
Humor them for their lunacy
Humor them in pretence
And on your face let a shadow overlay
The scorn; and offer no recompense
They are not champions
Of democracy and peace
Like Caligula they fornicate with their souls
And willingly they would sell their body
To find the kind of release
Only harlots and whores
With unshaken jowls
Can fool you with similar story

Too much hate
Reinforced by Ecclesiastes 3:1-8
Now it's my turn and your right

Ask them how they sleep at night
Through 'lies, lies, and damned lies'
The sanctity of life it defies

Too much hate
Stop
Before it's too late

Strive for peace
Remember Spinoza:
> *Peace is not the absence of war;*
> *it is a virtue;*
> *a state of mind;*
> *a disposition for benevolence;*
> *confidence;*
> *and justice."*

Mothers Children Missiles

I think of Spring   birds
soaring in the clearings   between
lush verdant trees
butterflies and other   lively
creatures of the Earth
embracing Nature in joyous mirth.

The children too   innocent broad smiles
show their open happiness   content
without bogus beguiles.
And mothers watchful   cavorting
with frivolous protective intent
their offspring
the envy of other mothers   they think.

I think of Iraq   the children
with faces lean and gaunt
whose mothers restraining smiles
contemplate horror of coming missiles
in the dark
that will wipe away children's bashful beam   the spark
of innocent light to be extinguished. Never
to hunger again in the covetous ephemeral ether...

Sacrilege

Who are we to even think   that
another person's life is worth_less?
That our land is the land of god   blessed
more than the land of others?
And our children have special dispensation
ordained by special creation
not given to the subaltern?

We demonize to hurt   to subjugate
to satiate our arrogance   to obfuscate
to justify our greed
and rob those in need.

The children of violence and those born in war
also smile   feel the pain   and cry
more than their mothers
who speak to the same god from afar.

Now your minds closed   detached
harsh   dry   cold
the desert sandy storm
the earth parched
the dry chaff. Behold!
All preferred to your litigation.
In the name of your god   a sacrilegious transgression.

Gary Girdhari

Bombs to end my hunger

Tell me not that you are a man of honor
When you send your bombs to end my hunger.
Tell me not that you are full of love
When your warplanes fill the sky above.
Tell me not that you care for me and my soil
When all you want is the forbidden oil.
Tell me not, [with] mournful numbers
When [their] souls [are] dead [in their] slumbers.

(Inspired by Henry Wadsworth Longfellow: A Psalm of Life.)

Schadenfreude

People:
It's people we're talking about
It's people   *people*
Human beings
    with faces   names
Not nameless
Blood runs thru their veins
    just like yours
They are children   mothers   fathers
Brothers   sisters   aunts   uncles
    like yours
With feelings and emotions
and needs
    just like yours.

You wont hurt a doggie
    or a kitten
    or a bird
Would you?

Why do you hurt them…
    those like *your* children   mothers   fathers
    brothers   sisters   aunts   uncles…
        Why?
                Why
won't you stop?

Schadenfreude? No!

Unwillingly Martyred

the night tired
the departed moon and eerie darkness
found hate in hands hired
lurking in the streets of terror
shattering the stillness
deafening, the blast   in horror
like all the bombs in the world   together
for a moment absorbed in the bones
waves of shock piercing the mind senseless forever
a temporary reprieve from the hell
created that moment   that night
when hate roamed the streets and minds as well.

the twilight   interlude till death
took him out of his turmoil
mind blanketed   wandering mind
flickering glimpses of light
reminding him in the hazy chaos
of the senseless separation
    four young ones and wife
grappling tenuously for the final breaths of life.

many tormented days and hours
the cowardly act did bring
and unwillingly martyred Seudyal Singh*
the Nation knee-jerked to reality
in shame, in recognition of human frailty.

*A security guard who was killed in Guyana, 1998

Philosophical

Knowing others is intelligence;
knowing yourself is true wisdom.
Mastering others is strength;
mastering yourself is true power.

Lao Tzu

My Psalm of Life

What is life if we do not care?
if we are mute out of fear?
To stand idle and just stare
is failure I do declare.

Unfading Footprints

It's good to walk the trodden path
looking for sign posts
of a memory   essential   to perk up
the ephemeral spirit

Footprints on that path...
Will they ever wash away?
Will they ever fade
as time pales the images?

Nay

Footprints mark the immortality
of those who tread there
like fossils of eons gone

Footprints, even if but a memory
are good and gratifying

Footprints never fade away
or wash away
in the temporal reality
or in the continuum beyond.

Gary Girdhari

The Law of Nature

The beaten path weathered, whether
    past or present, generation after generation
Many footprints on top of the other
Like microscopic slices of sedimentary formation.

You know that you've trampled the path of many
    family and friends
Transient, unpredictable with certainty, it's not uncanny
Like parents, grandparents, relatives   all depends.

Still, you're lucky that your footprints, you pray
    not yet fossilized in sedimentary formation
You look on in perplexed anticipation . . .
Like crests of tall trees awaiting the first light each day.

You become the forebears of those with new footprints
    smothering yours   now faintly bright; surely
    making them part of that sedimentary plane
Thus, to dust, destiny, the inevitable domain.

Transcendence and impermanence. It's the law of Nature
    replacing, revolving, not depleting   the continuum dictator
The reason for wonderment and expectation
Welcoming new footprints, with benign satisfaction.

(Written for Maia; 03/09/1998)

John Paul

The Pope is dead
Long live the dead!
The Vatican story fills the news
The senses bombarded with senseless abuse

John Paul is great, man from Poland
Enduring politics he began
This Pope, modern-day Superman
Politician, traveler, messenger to distant land

The long history of the Vatican
Secrecy of the papacy
Shroud the true story
Try as hard as you can

Wealth hidden from public eye – immense
Cruelty of the Inquisition
Can't be cleanse with ritual and incense
No apology, nay, not without due dispensation.

The Dearly Departed

As the end of the millennium draws near
Many souls, great and dear
Are taken through that revolving door
Making our earth more lonely and poor.

Within the past year or two
Death took its toll on many
But especially the champions   it's uncanny
Gratefully, they are but a few.

We always miss those who are great and good
For rights, justice and bread, they stood
Unwavering, these men and women, towering tall
Some with practiced ease, others with backs to the wall.

The world mourn them, their work still undone
Yet we cherish the fruits of vision they begun
We comfort ourselves with some surety
That their names are destined for posterity.

We remember

Paul Erdos of Hungary, genius of discrete mathematics
Carl Sagan, the American story-telling astronomer
The former "stripped himself of all the quotidian burdens of life"
The latter brought the stars and planets to scientists and commoner.

Jacques Cousteau, French explorer cajoled the world government
Because of his insights and dying concerns of the environment
Michael Manley and Cheddi Jagan, Caribbean leaders we lament
Their indomitable free spirit, full of good intent.

Betty Shabazz and William Brenner, advocates extraordinaire
Both Americans distinguished for a cause   to be fair
Nusrat Fateh Ali Khan, Pakistani musician with a different view
Brought *qawwali* out of the esoteric to the world anew.

Princess Diana, British, young, mother of future king
Touched the common, death to an anachronism may bring
Teresa, Mother of the teeming poor, needy and suffering
Extraordinary, Nobel Prize and Honors for self, means nothing.

(Written in 1997)

Procrastination or hypocrisy?

There is a lightness in my head
That causes my thoughts to wander
A lightness that soars even when in bed
The reason for my heart to go asunder.

I feel the pain, the agony, deep inside
The turmoil in the world that's gone mad
The challenge is not to put it aside
For this is what makes me really sad.

Good people, I know, say, they're sorry
When the deed is done and the horror seems to pass
They regret, they say, and this they carry
Till another day, when they repeat the same story.

I tell you my friend: you will not be spared in the end
For life is a complex blend of concordant diversity
And to the end, the beginning shall become the end
The final moment that unanticipated karmic or cosmic destiny.

Life's Conundrum

to die...
should be for me a moment of passionate rapturous joy
a joy_ful – full of life; my life like a buoy
bubbling with honeysuckle and jasmine
and lushness of memories sublime
the organic smell of just cut grass
and fresh cow dung   i pass
rotting jamoons squirting between gnarled toes …
forgetting sadhana turmoil and daily woes
these   the memories like an eternal fire
is my impassioned desire
when i yield to the reincarnate destiny
as my flame fades into infinity

soliloquy

is this sojourn the end on the ~~temporal~~ terrain
or the investiture into a revolving never-ending boundless domain?

Sadhana – Sanskrit: spiritual practice to achieve something, leading to dispassion
and non-attachment, when bondage becomes liberation.

Waiting and Wanting

I sit alone, here
In a reverie
Stargazing the firmament, and everywhere
The chair nearby is empty
c'est la vie.

Forsaken

The robin flirts on the branch
Now I see: they are a pair
(I wonder)
Why aren't you here?

Gary Girdhari

Will the yearning stop

Memory in perpetuity
or short-lived?
Will I always remember
like the salmon in spawn
or like the mayfly?
Is there only one meeting in this lifespan?

Dionysian delusion

It

> Cheers you up
> Heightens your emotions
> Dulls the senses
> Distorts reality
> Imbibed by scoundrels and saints
> By deadbeats and poets
> By the jilted and by lovers

It

> I imbibed tonight
>   to dull the senses
>   to blur a reality
>   to help my s l u m b e r
>   deeply and quickly
> Hoping to drown my roving thoughts
>   into forgetfulness.

Peace

Your stillness   your serenity
A moment of bliss to cherish till eternity
The lone dove is my silent witness.

alone

alone
loneliness
lonely
alone
fear
fearful
fearfulness
alone
bored
boredom
boring
alone
scared
scary...
and scorned
alone
fright
frightened
frightful
alone
lost
losing...
lifelessness
alone
dying
death
dead

thus   to dust
alone

Note: When I was writing this I was reflecting on the life of my mother, but also
considered, generally, the fragility of life and the certainty of death for all.

Gary Girdhari

Death

Where art thou?
Why?
Oh Yama! Why would you intercede
    in the samsara of my existence
        to rob me of the joy
that I've (was) created
    for me, and for my children
    and my grandchildren
    and their children
    and their grandchildren?

Are you telling me
    that you are the ultimate
        Decider
                of my fate?
That my mortal being
temporal, ephemeral
    is a wink
        in the span of time?

Or
Are you telling me, Oh Shiva
that you are the will of the Way
and thy bidding
    is congruous with the plan
        that is a continuum?

Yama: (Hindu) god of death.
Samsara – sanskrit: "continuous flow" – the cycle of birth, life, death and rebirth.
Shiva: (Hindu) Destroyer; also god of mercy and compassion.

Darkness

darkness tells its own story
when the mind's eye
takes over
the emotions   suppressed
spills out unabated   shameless
the truth   *in vino veritas*
deep in the lonely night
when nature goes to sleep
there is turmoil in my gut
like mount vesuvius expurgating
heat   pressure   fire
buried deep
in the private recess of the heart
offering cathartic release
the shanti shakti yogic harmony
bringing sanity   purity
seeking consciousness   reality
existential   atmic   eternal demand
the sat-chit-anand.

Sat-Chit-Anand: (hinduism) Truth-Consciousness-Bliss.

Dualism

Order and disorder
Consonance and dissonance
Change and stability
Destruction and creation
Uniformity and diversity
Oneness and plurality
Movement and constancy
Homogeneity and heterogeneity
Equilibrium and disequilibrium
Antinomies and compatibilities
Structured and amorphous
Rupa and *sunyata*
Spontaneous and premeditated
Congruence and chaos
War and peace
Convergence and divergence
Parallelism and causality
Euclidean and fractal
Randomness and self similarity
Rationality and illogicality
Metaphysics and dialectics
Empirical and hypothetical
Yin and yang
Youth and old age
Sadness and joy
Fullness and hunger
Life and death.

Seva

Give from the heart
From birth till you depart
Serve not to expect
In return only respect
Pray not for personal gain
Bribing god gives more pain
Say not it's my turn

Giving   serving   praying
Expect nothing in return

This is seva.

Seva: In Indic dharmic religions – service to God = selfless service to humanity.

Gary Girdhari

Pleading

I do not hope to return again
So let these words answer
What is done, is done
Not to be done again
May your judgment of me
and mine of you
not be too burdensome for you or me.

(Adapted from TS Eliot)

138